ISLINGTON

Islington Libraries

020 7527 6900   **www.islington.gov.uk/libraries**

FINDERS
KEEPERS

FINDERS
KEEPERS

POEMS
HARRY MAN

ILLUSTRATIONS
SOPHIE GAINSLEY

sidekickBOOKS
www.sidekickbooks.com

First published in 2016 by
SIDEKICK BOOKS

www.sidekickbooks.com

Printed by
ImprintDigital

Typeset in Vollkorn
Sidekick Books logo font: Roman Antique

Cover design by Jon Stone

ISBN: 978-1-909560-22-2

Supported using public funding by
ARTS COUNCIL ENGLAND
LOTTERY FUNDED

contents

introduction

"We have now acquired a fateful power to alter and destroy nature. But man is a part of nature, and his war against nature is inevitably a war against himself."

– *RACHEL CARSON*

Y OU DON'T have to travel very far to hear something from the English collective memory of the natural world. Although neither of us are ecologists, we wanted to capture some of these lives before they left, and this pamphlet was the net. We stayed in Britain, because when it comes to endangered species, it's not only the white rhino, the Sumatran tiger, or the Amazonian river dolphin that are under threat; it's also the cuckoo, the dormouse, and the salmon that are disappearing. It has not been an easy task, and if ever you want a fast way to wreck a pair of boots, rip a hole in your jacket, or become stranded in the sock-soaking rain on Exmoor, then this is probably the gig for you. Paradoxically there is little else that is as profoundly fulfilling.

There are 1,500 UK species on the International Union for the Conservation of Nature's protected red list, which means that they have been identified as endangered and are subject to a biodiversity action plan. This is split into research and monitoring, consultancy and advocacy, and policy and action. We have used the IUCN list as our guide, as well as opting for other species which spoke to the theme, or because on an expedition, that particular creature was all anyone wanted to talk about.

The Global Taxonomy Initiative estimates that there are between 5 and 30 million species around the world that have yet to be identified; globally we have identified 1.78 million species, meaning that even our most conservative estimate doesn't get us to the halfway line. Of those we have discovered, however, the central argument is not about conserving the species themselves, but protecting, and in some cases restoring, the diminishing number of wild places they inhabit. The Office of Natural Statistics values the contribution that nature makes to the UK economy at £1.2 trillion a year, and 60% of all our native species are in decline

These pages represent a broader series of conversations with landowners, lorry drivers, dog-walkers, gardeners, birdwatchers, artists, ramblers, curators, protesters, zookeepers, translators and teachers, amateurs and experts up and down the country who have made it their business to help conserve Britain's endangered wildlife, and to whom we are, all of us, greatly indebted.

HARRY MAN, North Yorkshire, 2016

MUCH of my artwork questions our attitude towards the natural world. I think fundamentally our arrogance as a species, combined with destructive powers from the recent industrial and technological ages, has done the most damage to our natural world. What we don't realise, as we plunder the oceans, continue to burn dirty, outdated energy in the form of fossil fuels, pollute the land and seas and clear forests, is our heavy dependency on these ecosystems for our own survival as a species.

It is precisely our fondness for fossil fuels and a fast pace of life which has eaten up much of the natural landscape and habitats on which the species we know and love depend. Forests, one of our biggest allies in the fight against anthropogenic climate change, are being cut down too quickly for creatures to adapt and find new homes. Some 46-58,000 square miles of forest are lost each year. This is equivalent to 48 football fields every minute. It is claimed that as much as half of the world's tropical forests have already been cleared. Mass mono-culture agriculture is playing a huge part in this, even here in the UK, as forests and wildflower-filled meadows are levelled to make way for single-crop fields. Our bees have suffered in particular.

But there is much we can do to help protect the creatures of our own little island ecosystem. The scale of this issue can seem daunting, but when you tackle extinction one species at a time and climate change one source at a time, the problems become a lot more manageable. I have been a climate and art activist for three years now. As my involvement in the divestment movement and the world of climate activism has taught me, it is easy to make a difference – a huge difference! You just need people and passion, and if you look around your local area, you are sure to find groups of people trying to make the world a better place in one way or another. Travelling around, even just within London, I always find plenty of people campaigning and fighting for positive change.

SOPHIE GAINSLEY, London, 2016

acknowledgements

Thank you to the editors of the following journals and websites where some of these poems have previously appeared: *Garo Station*, *Days of Poetry Famagusta*, *DancePoetry*, *Magma*, *Enchanting Verses Literary Review*. I am very grateful for the support of Arts Council England for a 2014-16 bursary, for the support of the Versopolis Project, and for the UNESCO Bridges of Struga Award 2014.

Thanks to the International Union for the Conservation of Nature, The People's Trust for Endangered Species, The Bat Conservation Trust, The British Council, The International League of Conservation Writers, The Laser Interferometer Gravitational Wave Observatory Collaboration, The Austrian Cultural Forum, Abigail Parry, Alex Anstey, Alice Oswald, Andy Willoughby, Annie Rutherford, Arvon Foundation, Ben Johncock, Beste Sakallı, Bob Beagerie, Claire Collison, Claire Trévien and Carlos the Amazing, Clare Pollard, Edward Brooke-Hitching, Eleanor Livingstone, The Fleetwood Initiative, Gareth Lewis, Glyn Maxwell, The Hawthornden Fellowship, Hannah Lowe, Heidi Williamson, Holly Corfield Carr, Jodie Hollander, Matt Bryden, Niall Munro and Nadia Arbach and Freida, Nikita Lalwani, Philippa Milnes-Smith, Richard Kerridge, Roddy Lumsden and The Lambeth Walk Workshop Group, Ros Wynne-Jones, Saradha Soobrayen, Sarah Hesketh, SJ Fowler, Sophie Gainsley, StAnza Poetry Festival, Tipping Point, Tom Moglu, Tom Weir, Andy Willoughby, Will & Sarah, friends and family and those I have missed, and Jennifer Essex.

Special thanks to Kirsten Irving and Jon Stone for introducing us to each other in the first place and for their tireless hard work and patience.

Diffusion

"The kind of motion it performs has often been compared with that of a blindfolded person ... changing his line continuously ... this random walk of the permanganate molecules, the same for all of them, should yet produce a regular flow towards the smaller concentration and ultimately make for uniformity of distribution."

From *What is Life?* by Erwin Schrodinger

A blindfolded man is walking across   a   field.

There is no wind.

Another blindfolded man   arrives.
The sun is overhead.

There is no wind.

A third blindfolded man is now   walking.

The barley feels the same against the legs.
The sun is overhead.

There is no wind.

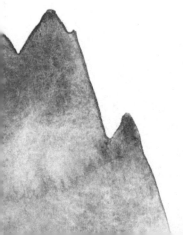

Here, a fourth blindfolded man.

The field is turning a rich purple.

The barley feels the same against the legs.
The sun is overhead.

The wind? No wind.

The blindfolded men smell permanganate.

The field is becoming a rich purple.

The barley feels the same against the legs.
The observer is overhead.

There is no wind.

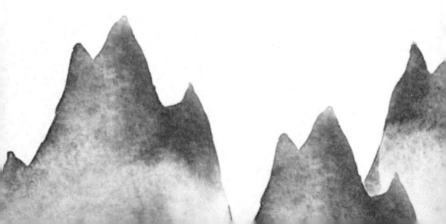

The blindfolded molecules are evenly distributed.

The field is a rich purple.

The molecules feel the same against the particles.
The observer is overhead.

There is no wind.

Schrödinger says, *First sight is perplexing, but only at first sight*.

We move from higher concentration to lower.

We close our eyes.

Purple.

There is no wind.

We are the observers in the wind.

The sun is in our head.

We imagine permanganate against our legs.

Our thoughts are evenly distributed.

The Gekkering

Lights off at Elmie's fried chicken shop,
      a shout, a double-take of noise in the polythene
           of the building site opposite, more of a howl –

a vixen calls out, the echo skims its double on the return,
      sticky rib bones in next door's garden, cider bottle caps.
           A lapwing watching the curl of the street is astonished

by nothing, now nothing can be heard and not seen.
      We fall for the fox's howl and howl, the howl
           as much for refuge as territory, as summoning,

piercing the navel, the night bus stesh stesh
      cutting the engine in Streatham garage water –
           the howl, this howl like a toddler longing now

for what possible logic might lie behind leaving,
      a thirsty Alsatian for its rotting owner,
           ranging the human nerves for every colour of fear.

Around her haunches a sodden newspaper
      and from her reflex, breath that parts over
           the algae on the white plastic water slide.

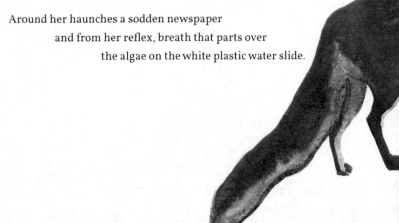

Shiverless, her fur wettens steadily
in the empty kind of rain that is either falling
or landing. In the near-blue of the grey

the sudden colour lit by kitchen lights
downstairs where our neighbour uselessly shoos
through the living stencil of his own reflection,

the needle-thin hair, the auburn fox-form of her;
a muzzle stiffening to a blurred bright world
to yield to whatever will tread for her

from the black perimeter; some spirit of foxness,
some colossus of fox, gigantic as an AM carrier wave,
grawking through the carpark, splitting the sheath,

the luxury concrete, fur trickling with brick dust and sparks,
teeth like the splitting of railings, here to gekker
the sleep-deprived out of their cotting
and the earth.

To gekker – To make a series of stuttering throaty vocalizations in
the manner of a fox when encountering a rival.

II

This Time

You bring the North Sea,
a tern's hunt, a fingerful of horizon

eddying under the surf
the bladderwrack riff,

salmon that dare a drive
so far from home for their young,

shiny handfuls of runaway
breath into breath, *all this time*.

Wombat 50,000

No gravitational credit to all you have undergone,
Humans process marsupials, and diprotodons' skeletons,
Australia dwarfs both terrestrial lizards and cousins
And sometimes birds die out in their tonnes and tonnes.
All top predators face competition and even I, in this,
Discovering your continent – for all that exploration – jar,
Myself coming, you going back to your cave, amiss,
I am coining the term 'dinosaur' more than your rhinos are.
As to your huge pouch, I respectively correspond.
Your sort of giant goose is your glacial maximum,
And under that much larger sea of self I glaciate.
Such sheer size was in my artist's impression,
That I, a protruding tooth, am sent all the way back
To my chain of islands, one gigantic empty nest.

Shakespeare's Sonnet 35 translated using text from 'Lost Giants' in
The Wonders of Life by Professor Brian Cox and Andrew Cohen.

Oak Mining Bee

"When I carry myself high, and the whole company
bow quiet before me, their blessedness
shall flourish skyward beneath my fostering shade."
> – From the Anglo Saxon 'Riddle to an Oak Beam'

tough-meadower
fall-crester
ball-wrecker
rush-golder
tree-colourer
sweet-homer

High Brown Fritillary

"I'm really an animal guy. I express myself in different ways as an animal."
    – Justin Bieber

I

Up with the birds, down with the kids,
halfway through the best of the violets,
you know how they get at that size.

The walk of a pantomime horse,
all bracken and prolegs and spines,
eating for the origami flying self.

Every caterpillar is a teen messiah;
look in on the twelve-eyed face,
the hungry religious indifference.

Crossing the knot of a hand
the teeth of a living cog can retract.

Playing dead, you can be out
for the count, dead to the world,
up with the birds, down with the kids.

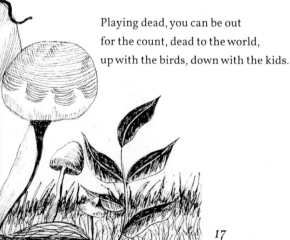

II.

Get to know the can-can,
fly religiously, an origami bird
like the back of your hand.

Size up, face down, kids count on
you living by your word,
to know the can-can.

Halfway caterpillar along the strand,
all drinking indifference is blurred,
never cog the back of your hand.

In the best horse bracken in the land
pros pantomime, the peacock unheard,
get to know the can-can.

Retract your legs from the stand,
cross the spines that you've spurned
like the back of your hand.

Play down the come-again plan,
knotted up in a beak you're absurd,
get to know the violet of the can-can,
the twelve eyes on the back of your hands.

At Home with a Hyper-Evolved Dormouse at Christmas

Few of us can hold up a paw in all honesty,
and say we've branched out enough
to try to understand the pound-sized humans
and what they get up to in our nation's woodlands.

At Christmas, having nibbled away at too much
organic goliath beetle and seen the Queen's squeak,
and after one too many berry liqueurs and sleepy,
I ditched the family to watch a documentary on the Beeb.

Filmed from a camera disguised as a caterpillar,
here we catch sight of a scuttling bearded male.
He sweats to hold a hazelnut fat as his own head,
heaving it up, up into the tops of a hedgerow and there,

upsetting the picture, a buzzard's adjusting wings
enfold him, his nut toppling to a thud
like the victim's pocket watch in a country house murder
as the bird rises, one hairy leg kicking from its beak.

Gulped down somewhere over Loughborough,
he's just another casualty of the fearsome power of nature.
Cut to a hole in the bark, the human's widowed mate –
she looks so tiny for forty-five seasons in the wild.

She will have to fend all autumn for her young.
Each baby is as small as a blackberry seed,
talk about long odds. The narrator is not hopeful.
I switch off the telly to write my thank-yous.

Now I've sent cards to Uncle Mart, and my sister Fay,
all with humans on the front, sniffing around the holly,
beady-eyed as criminals – the estate's about the litter,
not me, someone ought to do something, step in.

Bat Stance

On the backscattering echoes moths are quiet as bollards,
next to the half-shut shutters, pillars of Lavazza chairs,
the criss-crossed arch of an orb-weaver's web,
tuning each radial, levitating line in the wind.

Greylag geese, split figures-of-eight, swim over the arms
of a Bratz doll, cellophane, *Guaranteed Fresh for 7 Days.*
London's emergency services drench the scene,
bats come a way away in the sycamore ultramarine.

A lacewing by phonelight, a human face, says, *Oh
no I never, no I never ever*, as if *now* had more meaning than
then. Ian, a parks officer, eyes closed to re-memorise
shy to speak as the dead channel of radio fells us.

*Imagine being one kissing-quiet bat
what you could visualise; weigh each word
as it emerged, hear every earthly kind of satellite.*

The Lichen Last Seen in 1982

(Acarospora subrufula)

                                        ah
                                        ok

                            the colour
                                of Top
                         Secret ink
                      glistens,
                            the alkaline moonmarks bond
                            forms, web the ice segregated
            in   the   strata. No photogenic
                      lichen make headline
                      reading, a cheetah on
                            the kill,
                                  everything in focus,
                            Wildlife Photograph
        of the Year   or whatever, lichen drink
        like watching a   kettle, do you know that
        phrase? I suppose   you're too young
        to know   it. You won't see
                      a   bead of water sip-sipped,
                                  disappear. A photo-
                            biont has an alga brother,
                            the twig turned over
                      crazy paving, *is that what made*
                you take the house? And on your desert
                      island, you'll have Shakespeare and 8
              records. These cortices are tough as old boots.
          Behind the shared sugar rush these guys are all
    hardened users, bouncing off the walls; air pollution, so
          many idle engines, industrial pollutants kill
                off a lot, a lot of lichen – they look
                      hardy, but not so. If you care
              about antibiotics, say, or your cardy's colour…
    lichen do all of that and more. Shorelines, lowlands
    moors, churches,   way   sides,   varieties all over.

A Whale of a Time

I just don't feel the same way about you,
he tongues his baleen plates as if ready

to sing something into the open silence, but
he rests his throat grooves on his fin, looks

out of the rectangular window of the cable car
where the mist has made the Austrian valley seem

submerged. I realise we are committed to this.
Going anywhere nice this summer? I ask softly,

thinking of the 15,000 mile annual trip
to the Dominican Republic that he usually takes

with his whale friends. *We've only just met –*
the doughnut sugar tubercles bristle on his lips –

so I feel you could do with someone who was
I don't know, a good swimmer, a good role-model.

He snorts, so it rains. *Bubble-netting,*
that's a fun thing to do, provided you avoid

all those crab pot lines, and the shipping lanes,
and all of those camera crews coming out to see you.

He sings a high short note, a long slow moan.
It deepens into a wet farting balloon sound.

I know he will only repeat himself.
I open Google Translate, *Whale detected,*

it says, followed by, *What is your obsession*
with settling down? I thought we were having
a good time.

27

Norfolk Hawker

"The Norfolk Hawker is a delight to study. This is because places that are good for Norfolk Hawkers are also good for other species of dragonflies, notably Hairy dragonfly, Scarce Chaser and Variable Damselfly"

– Field Guide to the Dragonflies and Damselflies of Great Britain and Ireland.

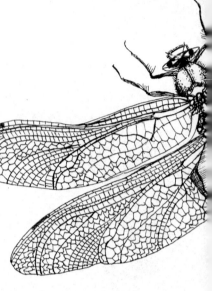

Hello, hello, look at the size of that Devil's Darning Needle
    which, like a lack of sleep, will tack and tack
from your double take. Such darters, hoverers, skimmers, chasers,
    fly like a flag that flaps in four directions.

You know 350 million years ago they survived
    our beginnings as moron amphibians;
we were scarcely out of the water when
    these poster-tubes were whizzing around.

Spindly little chaps their larvae are, though
    they have a chip on their shoulder;

they will try to eat anything and that can be their un-   doing.
We must stay low and still and slow and   they see you

long before you see them –   just there
she's landed in the water soldiers' longer leaves.
Fully grown there's a ginger glint
to their wishing-well-penny skins.

You can become quite obsessed quite quickly.
The upturned exuvia is a perfect perspex replica.
Imagine one of these decoys, it'd be prisoner's delight.
See you over the pond, by the wind-secluded water's edge,

or free at last; to bank and twist and hunt in Brampton Wood,
Pip-pip like Pinewood's pilots, *Good Luck*,
leave the uncanny cases to go for a Burton
on August's storms' damn, blast and double blast.
For any of you Norfolk Hawkers still alone along the broads
your exhibition cases are the stuff of natural history.

River Lamprey

"a ring, a watch, a locket,
Would drain at once a Poet's pocket;
He should send songs that cost him nought"
　　　　　– 'To a Young Lady, With Some Lampreys', John Gay

In one of Drax Power Station's filters are the sliced up dead
bucketed for carp bait.

Down-country is a kid in a PARENTAL ADVISORY
EXPLICIT CONTENT sweatshirt two sizes too big,

an old cassette tape ribbon in his hand
scribbling into the dark.

The tangerine of the Overground the ASH MEAT &
FISH CENTRE

the display grass and refrigeration, the emptiness
of trays which celebrate their emptiness.

In clear waters the river lamprey stack stones
like the men at war they never became

swim and let swim.

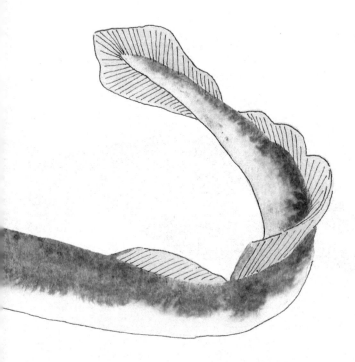

Great Crested Newt

Arms by my side I flew through life from the hatch,
trickled the furrows, the cool breeze of the current,
learned to think in the colours of your dream.

With the paramedic mastery of returning love
I will fold down the grass to cover our children,
unshroud myself from water, the mercury

drops of rain by security light, caddisflies too.
All I ever needed from this world was
a little wriggle room, another life in theory.

Dunlins

after dunlins – so many
white bellies constellate along the water's
jogged mirror,
and near, and across the 'No Mooring' sign
where I found – mysteriously – part of a car stereo,
the knocking ribs, the metronomic masts, and surf
and back
to roost together.

Years before, both fifteen, she pulls my hand
holding holding-still as best I can, to her waist –
warmness through her borrowed sweater
writing her number in blue biro, digit by firm, ovular digit,
how I was too shy to ever call
how all of that happened on this reserve.

The dunlins roll by again;
one of the flock is blown all over in the tightness of her toppling turn,
to you or me a couple of thousand feet in the air or more,
clenches her wings, again, again, again,
again and, once more,
in a startling arc of the purest kind of dare.

field notes

1. What is Life?

In Erwin Schrödinger's 1944 book, *What is Life?* the physicist describes how the universe is moving from a highly ordered state to a more chaotic state, and how this entropy is like diffusion, ie. it spreads. Where there is life, there is negative entropy; we create alloys and we build houses and schools, so things become more ordered and the world around us more regular. In the same way, animals will build nests, create burrows and construct dams; these are the hallmarks of negative entropy. On an atomic scale, the world is far less ordered, and the movements of atoms more chaotic, but at a classical level in the tangible world around us, there is a great deal of order – the chair remains solid as we go to sit down. To put it another way, in the comfort of our human lives, we are limited in our view as to what is static and what is being lost. In the same book, Schrödinger also presents his view on how genetic information might be stored. This prompted the discovery of the helical structure of DNA which is present in all life on Earth.

2. Red Fox (Vulpes vulpes)

An old Breton folk tale tells the story of a young man who sets out on a quest to cure his dying father. On the way he spends all of his money on the funeral expenses of a stranger. He soon meets a fox which helps him in his quest with its advice. With his money gone, and against all odds, he finds the cure. Once the search is over, the fox transforms, revealing that it is the soul of the dead person buried by young man's charity. Then the apparition vanishes.

First colonising the city in the 1930s, around one third of all the urban foxes in the UK live in the boroughs of London. Despite appearances, the fox's relationship with the urban environment is a precarious one. In 1994 an outbreak of sarcoptic mange reduced the population of foxes in Bristol by 95% in two years. Around a quarter of all foxes in England die on the roads and the average life expectancy of a British red fox is eighteen months.

More information about the red fox, and facts and figures, as well as practical advice, may be found at www.thefoxwebsite.net and www.foxproject.org.

3. Atlantic Salmon (Salmo salar)

In Irish mythology, Fionn mac Cumhaill was under the tutelage of the poet and druid Finnegas. The story goes that Finnegas is in search of a salmon which has been feeding on sacred hazelnuts and berries. This special diet, Finnegas believes, will have transformed the otherwise ordinary fish into the Salmon of Knowledge. After seven years without any luck, one day Finnegas and Fionn are fishing together by the River Boyne, when all at once they see the signature eddy of the Salmon of Knowledge. They lower their rods and it swims towards them. Finnegas rushes for his net, bags the salmon, and tells Fionn to cook it, with strict instructions that Fionn shouldn't eat so much as a forkful. Finnegas leaves him to it. Obediently, Fionn gets the fire going, stoking the wood and turning the salmon, which is sizzling and spitting away. Before long, some of the hot oil from the salmon's skin spits and hits Fionn on the thumb. To relieve the pain, Fionn sucks his thumb. By so doing Fionn is suddenly overwhelmed, as all of the salmon's divine wisdom and all of its knowledge spills into him.

Most salmon offered for sale is farmed and the Atlantic salmon is the UK's favourite fish (source: Marine Conservation Society, 2016). Infectious disease and sea lice spread quickly on salmon farms, particularly where salmon are reared in cages, and the berries and hazelnuts of the Irish myth have been replaced by antibiotics and feed pellets made from corn, soy and the discarded remains of other fish. In the North of England, and further up into Scotland, where conditions are tougher, the climate colder, and terrain more mountainous, salmon tend to take longer to reach an age where they can smolt and migrate from river to sea. In Southern England it's a different story – salmon can smolt as yearlings. The biggest threat to populations is the high concentration of sea lice found among farmed salmon, which multiply in the confined conditions of sea-rearing cages. Salmon can be in cages with 70,000 other individuals, often more, and escapes are common. Once free, the larger farm-reared salmon will spread sea lice and interbreed with native salmon, making unviable offspring, and pushing the wild population to extinction.

The farming of Atlantic salmon seems to be short-term thinking in the extreme. Data published by *The Guardian* in 2012 shows a threefold increase in chemicals used in salmon farming in Scotland, where the industry is worth over £540 million. In some rivers, wild stocks have entirely collapsed. If you like to eat fish, the Marine Conservation Society have developed the 'Good Fish Guide' app for iPhone and Android to help you to make an informed decision about which fish to eat to minimise your impact on the environment. To find out more about the Atlantic salmon and how you can help, visit the Atlantic Salmon Trust at www.atlanticsalmontrust.org.

4. Diprotodon (*Diprotodon optatum*)

The diprotodon was an enormous wombat-like creature and the biggest marsupial ever to have lived. Diprotodon is so named for its two large front teeth. It consumed around 100-150kg of vegetation every day – the weight of a small upright piano. Having spent 1.6 million years in relative peace and quiet, the animal was hunted to extinction by our ancestors in around 44,000 BC. There is a very large diprotodon skeleton on display in London's Natural History Museum (www.nhm.ac.uk).

5. Oak Mining Bee (*Andrena ferox*)

Unlike the honeybee, the oak mining bee is not what is termed a 'social bee', meaning it has no hive, and so no interest in hanging around with tens of thousands of other bees. Instead it spends the majority of its time on the wing, or looking after its brood. The oak mining bee is not a honey producer but instead stuffs green and yellow pollen into the lining of its tracksuit-bottom-like hind legs.

The oak mining bee seems almost monastic, exclusively collecting pollen from the oak trees to which it has devoted its life, and its survival depends heavily on the success of this symbiotic relationship. There are 20 species of bee in the UK currently in active conservation programmes, including the large garden bumblebee, the brown-banded carder bee and the large mason bee. You can help solitary bees survive by building a brightly coloured (and thankfully not very complicated) solitary bee house. You can find instructions on how to do this on the Grow Wild UK website: www.growwilduk.com. To learn more about the different species of bees in your area, contact your local Wildlife Trust: www.wildlifetrusts.org.

When you first hear about the high brown fritillary's teenage years, you realise we have nothing to complain about. The high brown is a caterpillar well into middle age, during which time it is unable to reproduce and largely resembles a mouldy chocolate éclair. It lives out in the open, often around dead bracken, and in a state of semi-hibernation. It feeds on violets, before shedding its skin into a chrysalis, and in the ultimate act of teenage angst, going back to bed for a whole month or *WHENEVER, SHUT UP!*

The University of Manchester and the University of Bristol have both recently published computerised tomography (CT) scans showing the inner workings of the pupation process of different butterflies, revealing the transformation of internal organs, including the entire respiratory and digestive systems. What remains baffling to entomologists is that, despite this radical change in appearance inside and out, the genetic code has not changed – it's the same individual. One volunteer put it this way: "It's as if in goes a tea towel and out comes Wembley Stadium."

76% of all British species of butterfly were in decline between 2005 and 2015. The high brown fritillary, however, has rallied. After a 96% decline, populations are now up by 180%. The reasons for this bounce-back are grants and careful land management, as well as work by, among others, the charity Butterfly Conservation.

In a strange David-and-Goliath twist to the story, this delicate insect, little bigger than a folded train ticket, is reliant on the comparatively Godzilla-like wild ponies and cattle that nuzzle and trample down the shoulder-height bracken. This gigantic trampling opens up what must seem like great idyllic plains to the delicate butterfly. These plains are stocked with dead grass and bracken, and here violets can catch more than their usual glimmer of sunlight and grow. The high browns can then descend on their new-found territory and lay their eggs, which will one day hatch to become the loveably awkward, spiky, sleepy, middle-aged teenagers they always wanted.

Butterflies are cold-blooded and need to be heated to around 30°C before they can fly, which is why you often see them basking in the sun and turning toward the light. To find out more about butterfly conservation, to volunteer, or to take part in the annual Big Butterfly Count, visit www.butterfly-conservation.org.

7. Hazel Dormouse (Muscardinus avellanarius)

The Elizabethans once used dormouse body fat as a remedy for insomnia, and the Victorians, admiring the natural reticence to bite, kept dormice as pets. Each adult dormouse weighs around 15-25g (about the same as five sugar cubes) and has sandy, ginger fur and rose-petal-pink paws. When in torpor, the dormouse will tuck itself into a ball, eyes squeezed closed, with a fine bushy tail wound over its head, slowing its heart rate down to one beat every six seconds. For an animal with such a reputation for sleeping on the job, you would have thought they would make for terrible builders, but their home-spun nests of hazel leaves and honeysuckle bark are brilliantly neat. Females are better builders than males, who are sometimes found trying to get a good afternoon's kip under two twigs, with a leaf over the face – probably one found right by the back door. We were lucky enough to take part in a dormouse survey with the People's Trust for Endangered Species. You can find out more about dormice on the PTES website: https://ptes.org.

8. Common Pipistrelle Bat (Pipistrellus pipistrellus)

The pipistrelle gets its name from the Latin *verspetillo*, meaning 'evening bat', and is one of the world's smallest flying mammals. The common pipistrelle is almost identical to its sister species the soprano pipistrelle, so much so that they were only identified as being two separate species in 1999. The soprano has an echolocative call which is higher in frequency, hence the name. The common pipistrelle was the first creature we looked at, and although pipistrelles are not endangered, there are five other bats which are. They include the barbastelle, the Bechstein's bat, the brown long-eared bat, the greater horseshoe bat and the lesser horseshoe bat. If you were to create a family tree of all our planet's mammals, it might surprise you to learn that 20% of the entire tree would be made up exclusively of bats, making them the second most classified mammal on Earth (the first being rodents). We used bat detectors to hear the chittering of these bats over the radio, which sounds a little like someone blowing kisses into a mobile phone. You can have a listen to this noise, recorded on one of our expeditions, on the *Finders Keepers* website: www.finderskeepers.org.uk. The Bat Conservation Trust have recently launched *The Big Bat Map*, which allows you to see where bats have been spotted in your area, and to log your own sightings. To find out more about the work of the Bat Conservation Trust, or to build your own bat roosting box (to go with your solitary bee box; *see 5. Oak Mining Bee*) visit www.bats.org.uk.

9. Lichen (Acarospora subrufula)

In August 1928, while Alexander Fleming was on holiday, the bacteria *staphylococcus* was gradually being cultivated on petri dishes in his lab. The window having been left open, something blew in, landed on his petri dishes and began to grow into a mould. By an extraordinary stroke of luck this mould was creating a chemical compound that was highly effective at killing off the *staphylococcus*. Up until this moment, a simple bacterial infection from something as small as a paper cut could be lethal, and an infection caught on a Monday could kill you by Friday. Fleming recognised that, when isolated, this chemical might be used in medicine, but failed to appreciate the significance of his discovery: penicillin.

Twelve years later, Australian doctor Howard Florey and his team at the Oxford School of Pathology recognised the drug's potential in the war effort: to fight off infection among the wounded and send them back to the front. Before Florey and his team could conduct a human drug trial, they had to cultivate an awful lot more of this magical compound, which required a carefully controlled balance of oxygen and yeast. They ended up using bed pans and a milk churn, which they put on a bookshelf swiped from the Bodleian Library. Paris fell to the Nazis in June 1940 and the team knew that, should Germany invade Britain, they would need to destroy their work. As a precautionary measure, the team kept *penicillium* spores smeared on the insides of their overcoats. It is estimated that since its introduction, penicillin has saved around 200 million lives worldwide.

In 1942, the same year Fleming was appearing on the cover of *Time* magazine in America, five new strains of penicillin-resistant *staphylococcus* were identified. Today the fight for antibiotics has accelerated and infectious bacteria have become ever more resistant. One of the last hopes in the fight are the small lichens, discovered and undiscovered, around the country. To help fight the good fight, you can sign up to University College London's 'Swab and Send', a project which encourages members of the public to swab 'anywhere unusual' for bacteria, such as 'the inside of your hoover', which might just be generating a life-saving chemical compound.

There are 138 species of lichen on the IUCN red list, including the Arctic Kidney and the River Jelly. Although they lack the iconic status of the panda bear or the Christmas-card familiarity of the robin, the humble lichen might just be the key to our future survival. For more information about lichen, visit www.britishlichensociety.org.uk, and to sign up for UCL's Swab and Send scheme, head over to https://ucl. hubbub.net/p/swab-and-send.

10. Humpback Whale (Megaptera novaeangliae)

The name means 'The Big Wing from New England'. When humpbacks 'breach' (surface and plunge down into the waves), the bright, dappled white underside of their tails becomes visible, hence the name. The humpbacks' tails don't flap so much as collapse into the sea. They can weigh up to 50 tonnes. Compared to this animal, we are miniature. The four-chambered heart of an average adult humpback whale weighs 195 kilograms, which is about the same as a man, a woman, a teenager and his smartphone, or, to make things more interesting, 6,700 Valentine's Day cards or 3,000 tennis balls.

The humpback whale sings in what are called 'themes' – short phrases which are repeated over and again for anything up to half an hour. When one male finishes, another takes up the song, adding in notes and melodic flourishes. Sound travels more than four times faster through water (just shy of 1.5 kilometres per second), allowing humpback whales to communicate with each other over vast distances. It is possible then that humpbacks are aware of the geography of the world's oceans in a way that even our best satellite technology and sonar cannot match.

Humpback whales also hunt by creating bubble nets, where a pod of whales will encircle large quantities of herring with bubbles before taking it in turns to swim up through the centre, gulping down huge numbers of fresh, panic-struck fish. Looking out over a quiet, calm Norwegian inlet, you will hear what sounds like a cassette of the *Koyaanisqatsi* soundtrack being chewed underwater, before bubbles as big as footballs bulge and break on the surface, and quite suddenly thousands of herring leap like skipping stones every which way.

The humpback was once hunted to the edge of extinction, with an estimated population low of 700, until 1966, when a ban was introduced by the International Whaling Commission. Although global populations are now up to 80,000 individuals, this is still short of pre-whaling numbers, which are thought to have been around 125,000. To find out more about dolphin and whale conservation visit: uk.whales.org.

11. Norfolk Hawker (Aeshna isosceles)

Guessing the age of someone else and aiming for flattery, but ending in faux pas, is something the dragonfly will never have to worry about. The colour-detecting opsins (proteins) within a dragonfly's eye allow it to see more colours than we can, including ultraviolet. This ability means that it can tell the age of its fellow dragonflies before courting can begin, and it can see other insects very clearly against a strikingly luminescent sky. Like the Cupola on the International Space Station, the dragonfly has a 360° view of the world and space it is flying around and through. When the clouds clear, the view of the night sky seen in these additional pigments, including the ultraviolet spectrum, must be staggering, and it is something the dragonfly is able to take in night after night.

The Norfolk hawker (also known as the green-eyed hawker) lives on wetlands and spends three years underwater as an omnivorous larva before clambering onto low-lying vegetation and becoming a dragonfly for about eight weeks over the summer. Its Greek name, *Aeshna isosceles*, comes from an old misprinting of the Greek word *aechma*, meaning 'spear', and *isosceles*, meaning 'equal legs'. In this instance, however, *isosceles* was chosen in reference to the distinctive yellow triangle found on the lower abdomen.

Species of dragonfly are named after the way in which they hunt: varieties include skimmers, darters, hoverers, chasers, and hawkers. Hawkers hunt by making their six legs into a small basket and intercepting their prey – a midge or mosquito (or occasionally a butterfly or another dragonfly) – on the wing, before feeding it to themselves. The wetlands across places such as Wicken in Cambridgeshire are being restored, grazing marshes protected by the government, and the habitats of the hawker and around 25 other species of dragonfly that live in the region are being extended. The British Dragonfly Society is a font of knowledge, and their enthusiasm for their subject is second to none. They have also developed an app for identifying dragonflies in the wild, which is available through their website: www.british-dragonflies.org.uk.

12. River Lamprey (Lampetra fluviatilis)

There are three species of lamprey in the UK: the sea lamprey, the river lamprey and the brook lamprey. The river lamprey is a small, eel-like, primitive and rather slithery parasitical fish with a jawless, round mouth lined with teeth. If you look around the dinner table and think you recognise a few of its characteristics in other people, you're not so far from the truth. It is current scientific consensus that our ancient ancestors looked much the same way. The lamprey first evolved 400 million years ago, preceding the first dinosaurs by almost 200 million years. Most of the rest of its kind, the jawless 'agnathans', are no longer around, leaving the lamprey behind, a fish out of time.

Lampreys were regarded as a delicacy by the Romans and the Vikings, and on into the medieval period. The most famous story regarding lampreys in England is that of Henry I, the fourth son of William the Conqueror, who was said to have died from 'a surfeit of lampreys'. While in a hunting lodge in Lyons-la-Forêt, apparently excited for the hunt the following morning, Henry fell ill. Against his physician's advice, he had dined on lampreys, although Roger of Wendover noted: "They always disagreed with him ... this food mortally chilled the old man's blood and caused a sudden and violent illness against which nature struggled and brought on an acute fever." Within a few days he was dead.

Another English monarch, King John, often portrayed as the villain in the Robin Hood story, is said to have fined the City of Gloucester the equivalent of £250,000 for failing to deliver his Christmas lamprey pie. The city continued this tradition until 1836. Although made with imported and non-endangered Canadian lamprey, the lamprey pie continues its royal association to this day. The City of Gloucester supplied the Queen with their latest pie in September 2015 because, said Paul James of Gloucester City Council, "We couldn't let the occasion of Her Majesty becoming our longest-reigning monarch pass without marking it in this time-honoured way." The recipe for lamprey pie includes bacon, unsalted butter, onions, cream, potatoes and locally grown fresh herbs. Just be sure to use imported lamprey.

Lampreys are able to recover from spinal injuries that would leave a human paralysed, and because of our shared genetics, particularly in their central nervous system, lampreys are vital for research. Lampreys also serve an important role in the interlocking 'food webs' within British rivers, helping to process nutrients in the water, as well as providing a rich food source for birds like sawbill ducks and herons, and other fish. Thanks to a reduction in pollution, and the removal of artificial barriers such as weirs, river lamprey can travel upriver again, and their numbers are on the rise in rivers such as the Ouse and the Derwent. To find out more about river lampreys, and to support the health of British rivers, visit the Canal and River Trust: https://canalrivertrust.org.uk.

13. Great Crested Newt (Triturus cristatus)

The 'Parable of the Coffeepot Incident' is known to many herpetologists in the western United States. Deep in the Oregon woodland, three hunters are found next their tents, dead. Nothing seems out of place, no sign of an animal attack, their weapons are still in their zipped-up cases, and nothing to suggest a struggle. On the stove in the middle of the site is a single pot of coffee. Initially the authorities are mystified. Upon closer inspection of the coffee pot, in the dregs of the coffee, they find a single boiled newt. This story is told to warn children and adults alike that licking or tasting, or sometimes even just touching a newt is a seriously bad idea.

Its coiffured appearance (the males' crests are used for attracting females), together with its penchant for hanging around construction sites and eating smaller newts, make the great crested newt sound like some sort of gangster. At close range, however, it is a remarkably delicate creature, which, as it treads across your hand with its brightly coloured feet, feels like someone running a cold, wet finger along your palm. It is a playground sensation, as though you are the subject of some very special spell, or at the beginning of an adventure story. Turning the newt over, each one has a flash of bright orange on its belly, with a pattern of spots as unique as a fingerprint.

Victorian naturalist Eleanor Ormerod decided, "for the sake of ascertaining sensations", to put part of the back and tail of a live crested newt between her teeth:

"The first effect was a bitter astringent feeling in the mouth, with irritation of the upper part of the throat, numbing of the teeth more immediately [than] holding the animal, and in about a minute from the first touch of the newt, a strong flow of saliva. This was accompanied by much foam and violent spasmodic action, approaching convulsions, but entirely confined to the mouth itself. The experiment was immediately followed by [a] headache lasting for some hours, general discomfort of the system, and half an hour after by slight shivering fits."

Unfortunately, Eleanor Ormerod then decided to conduct the same test on her cat.

The great crested newt is heavily protected by the law, and disturbing them or their habitat can land you with an unlimited fine and a six-month prison sentence, as can 'possessing, selling, controlling or transporting live or dead newts, or parts of them'. When newts are found on a construction site, all construction must come to a grinding halt. The British answer to CSI pile out of the back of a minibus with their wellies on, packed lunches with Wagon Wheels, and tablet PCs in rubber weatherproof cases, to carry out a full survey of the newts on the site. Damage to the newt's habitat has to be mitigated, and this can leave developers with a hefty bill.

A fully grown great crested can be anywhere between 15 and 17cm long, and throughout the year their survival relies on the satisfaction of several different demands. For spawning, the newts require a fish-free (and hopefully duck-free) pond with just the right pH balance and amount of vegetation. This pond should be in a spot with a decent amount of sun, as their young, called efts, require a reasonably warm environment, and since they hatch in April, this is not always easy to come by. The efts make the transition from water-based larvae to adolescent punk-rocker land dwellers. They need plenty of shelter, such as abandoned mammal burrows, rubble or hollow logs. Occasionally these newts have been found under sheets of corrugated iron, which has helped to keep them warm and out of sight. Currently the main threats to newts are the pollution of their habitat by construction, intensive farming and habitat fragmentation. Great crested newts like to return to their spawning grounds, and will undertake long journeys to do so, even if at the other end there is nothing but a 'STUNNING NEW DEVELOPMENT' sign. According to the Freshwater Habitats Trust, around three-quarters of rivers and 90% of ponds in the UK are damaged by pollution, making freshwater wildlife one of the most threatened parts of the natural world. The Freshwater Habitats Trust works across research, policy, and practical and community projects throughout the UK, including conserving the habitats of the great crested newt. You can find out more about their work at www.freshwaterhabitats.org.uk.

14. Dunlin (Calidris alpina)

Sitting on a pebble beach close to the Isle of Wight, looking out over a salt marsh, suddenly the stones in my peripheral vision seemed to twitch and come alive. Very quickly, rising from the bricolage of smashed hulls and stranded, rusted iron came a crowd of these very small birds. The flocking pattern in which birds, particularly starlings, swirl and turn and come together is known as a murmuration. The word 'murmuration' may have its roots in the Sanskrit *murmurah*, meaning 'a rustling' or 'the crackling of fire', and as the wind picks up, it's easy to see the similarity between this flocking and the upward travel of ash from a fire. The dunlin has a light brown stripe on its back, and occasionally they stand close to flocks of feeding plovers, giving rise to the Scottish nickname for them, 'plover's page'.

The dunlin is not endangered, and is categorised by the IUCN as being of 'least concern'. It does, however, inhabit salt marshes, which are critically threatened habitats. These comprise intertidal mudflats and small, marshy lagoons which provide protection against flooding and rising tides. Around the northern edge of the Solent, where we were, is cordgrass, and this is the only place in the UK where it grows. In winter, grazed salt marshes are used as feeding grounds by large flocks of wild ducks and geese. The salt marshes are also important in providing nursery areas for commercial fish such as sea bass, which arrive like hungry, jet-lagged tourists from the sea, and, on arrival, eat over 8% of their own bodyweight in food in the first two hours alone.